MW01595151

# Agaayun Asirtuq

## God is Good

BY WINENE NIMMO

For my good
friend, Mary,
who spent many
years in Bethel
serving the Lord.
May you enjoy
and get a blessing
from reading this
book.
Heb. 13:20, 21
Love in Him,
Winewe Nimmo

# Agaayun Asirtuq

## God is Good

BY WINENE NIMMO

All Scriptures are taken from the King James Bible.

ISBN# 978-1-61119-053-3

Printed in the United States of America.

Printed by Calvary Publishing
A Ministry of Parker Memorial Baptist Church
1902 East Cavanaugh Road
Lansing, Michigan 48910
www.CalvaryPublishing.org

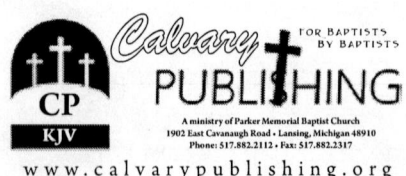

Calvary PUBLISHING
FOR BAPTISTS BY BAPTISTS
CP KJV
A ministry of Parker Memorial Baptist Church
1902 East Cavanaugh Road • Lansing, Michigan 48910
Phone: 517.882.2112 • Fax: 517.882.2317
www.calvarypublishing.org

## FOREWORD & ACKNOWLEDGEMENTS

First of all I would like to thank my husband, Fred, for his patience and encouragement. He also did some editing. (His memory is better than mine.)

My sister, Ranelle, did some editing for me as well. I am indebted to her. My friend, Evelyn Haxton, edited the manuscript in its early inception. Naomi Mathews helped me with some formatting problems. Later she tweaked the pictures to help make them look better. A big thank you is due her. Thanks to Linda Hammer for some final editing help that was really needed.

Jackie Oldfield of Post Falls, ID, designed the book cover for me. I will forever be grateful to her for the great job she did!

And, Norma Smith has been a great help in getting copies done. I thank her for all the hours she has put into it.

I would like to say that many of the pictures were converted from old slides to digital pictures. Because of this the quality is not really good. Some of them were originally taken during winter when sunlight was severely limited. I did a lot of working with them – but I do not have expensive equipment.

The inspiration to write my story came while reading Elmer Deal's book, Out of the Mouth of Lions. (He was a missionary in the Congo for over 50 years.) If you have not read his story, it is very good reading. My story is quite a contrast – from Africa to Alaska!

It is my prayer that this little booklet will be a blessing as well as entertaining.

If I have made mistakes, I am very sorry. Some of this happened many years ago; and with the passing of years, the memory fades.

*wn*

Maggie Lind, ptarmigan headband

My mukluks made by Mary Kuku, Annie Friendly's mother

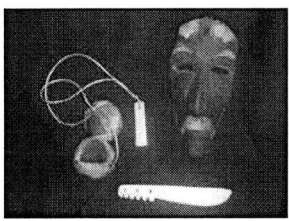

Yoyo by Lyda Iyakitan (St Lawrence Island), mask from Justus Mekianna (Anaktuvik Pass), old ivory story knife from Togiak (Dillingham area)

Ivory ship, Arnold Iyakitan, Eskimo doll (with story knife) given to us by Adolph Friendly

Birch bark basket given by Anna Anvil, back left (Athabaskan Indian work); sweet grass baskets given by Mrs. Jacobs from Hooper Bay. (The one on lower left is most unusual, with yarn woven in.)

## EARLY YEARS

I was born on December 28, 1937 on a farm north of Quanah, Texas near the Red River which borders on Oklahoma. My mother was Bessie Lorene (Hopkins) Herring and my dad was Winfield Samuel Herring. (My name is a combination of Winfield and Lorene.)

The story is told on my dad that on one occasion he and a few of his friends disassembled a Model T Ford and reassembled it on the High School stage. Everyone had a hard time figuring out how that car got on the stage! I don't remember being told whether he was disciplined or not.

Mother once had a pet mule. I have a snapshot of her sitting on the mule's haunches. Pet or no pet, I think she was much braver than I would have been. She also had a pet rabbit that she had taken from the field. She took care of it for some time. Even after she let it go again it would come and sleep under the porch. Mother always enjoyed the outdoors.

Mother's relatives were Southern Baptist and Dad's relatives were Methodist. I don't think his family ever completely forgave my mom for "making a Baptist out of him."

There were five children: three girls and two boys: Ranelle, Bennoit, Dennis, (Me), and Sharron. (I think my mother must have been reading a French novel to come up with the name of Bennoit for my brother.) Of course there was some fighting and usually someone ended up getting hurt. I watched the older siblings go to mother with loud crying and saying, "Dennis hurt me and he did it on purpose too!" One day I accidentally hurt myself. I went to mother and told her I had hurt myself and had done it on purpose too. I guess I thought that meant I was really hurting!

My dad was a farmer and I remember pulling bolls (cotton) at an early age. We used an orange bag, graduating to a gunny sack (which we called a toe sack), and finally to a 10 or 12 foot-long sack. One time I remember helping my sister finish her row of cotton. Both of our bags were so heavy we could hardly pull them. Then came a hissing sound and we saw a snake coiled up around a cotton plant nearby. We took off in all directions, pulling those sacks as though they were filled with feathers!

I remember another occasion when we were gathering eggs. My dad gave me two eggs to carry in my hands to the house. I began to run. While slinging my arms back and forth I let go of one of the eggs. It landed right in my father's face. He was NOT a happy camper!!

We did not have electricity or running water on this farm. One evening as we were all sitting around the table, Daddy suddenly picked up the oil lamp and threw it with all his might towards the door. It flew out the screen door and burst into flames. We thought Dad had gone crazy. We did not know that he had seen the wick going down into the oil and knew it was likely to explode any minute.

We had a family tradition about Christmas. On Christmas Eve the first one up went around telling everyone else, "Christmas eve gift." I guess that meant that we all should give that one a gift – but I don't recall that ever happening. One bright, cold Christmas day I do remember Dad getting each one of us up out of the bed and throwing us into a snow drift just off the front porch. What a rude awakening!!

For quite some time we drove from our farm near Quanah to Wellington, Texas, so that we could worship in an independent Baptist church. (My dad came to terms with the Southern Baptists when they told him he should teach his Sunday school lessons from the quarterly.) I think it was about 60 miles each way. Back then that was quite a drive; especially, when your car was not running well and a fire would develop under the hood. Dad would get out and throw dirt on it to stop the fire. I decided to help. I grabbed a handful of dirt; but, because I was so short I only managed to throw it on my dad's back. Of course, he was in his Sunday suit. So much for my help!!

Once after a service at the church in Wellington, TX, we were playing with the pastor's children. We were playing "Pop the Whip". I remember being carried along without my feet touching the ground. When we began to pop the whip, I was thrown very hard on my right shoulder. There was a pop all right. It was my collar bone. We drove back to Quanah and then stopped in at the hospital. We were told to come back in the morning. What a miserable night. The next morning we had x-rays done and found that my collarbone was broken.

At one point (when I was about 6 years old) my grandfather Herring was diagnosed with terminal liver cancer. Dad moved our family to a small house on grandfather Herring's large farm and dad helped out with the farm until my grandfather passed away.

One remembrance of that time was a huge overhead gravity flow shower. As I remember it was a rock building which stood off to itself. It was fed by water pumped by a windmill directly from the well. After a very hot day I would go in there for a very cold shower. It was really hard to stay under the cold water – but very refreshing.

Another vague memory is of hog-killing time. The hogs were dipped in vats filled with hot water, split open, and hung to bleed out. Several women would get together to make sausage.

My mother used to read to us in the evenings. Most of the books were Christian books with a missionary flavor. Sometimes she would read other stories as well. One story I remember well was about an old faithful horse on the farm. The family bought a nice, new shiny automobile. After that the horse was left in the barn, ignored and desolate. Finally one day the car got stuck in the mud and they had to get the horse to pull it out. I remember crying for the horse when he felt so deserted, but happy when he was the hero of the day by pulling the car out of the mud.

About this time my father surrendered to preach the gospel. He decided to enroll in Bible Baptist Seminary in Ft. Worth, Texas. My mother and we five children moved to Eldorado, Okla. (just across the Red River) to be near my grandfather and grandmother Hopkins. There I entered first grade. We then moved to Wellington, Texas; Quanah, Texas; and, finally Ft. Worth. This was all during my first grade of school.

In Fort Worth we lived just across the road from the Trinity River. We had many fun days swimming. One day we came home from school to a new bicycle in our front yard. We could not believe it was for us -- one bicycle for 5 of us to share. We were so proud of that bike. (This was during WWII, so money for toys was scarce.)

My brother, Dennis, liked to chase my sister and me with little green snakes he found near the river bank. Mother would spank him, but I think he enjoyed it so much he would endure the spankings!

Prior to living in Ft. Worth we had always lived on the farm or in a small town. We had to get accustomed to close neighbors. There was a couple next door, Johnnie and Sudie Bell, who were known to get drunk once in a while. None of us had ever heard any curse words, or seen anyone drunk. One day we were out in the back yard and they were going after it hot and heavy and using some colorful words. I remember mother coming out in the yard and telling us to come in the house. We had just been standing there with out mouths open wondering what was being said!

We were living in Ft. Worth when WWII ended. What a grand parade the children of the neighborhood had!! We marched up and down the street making noise with any kind of pot or pan and yelling, "The war's over, the war's over!"

With five children we were able to play different games such as baseball, volleyball, and basketball. Another pastime was to play "church". My brother, Dennis, would lead singing while my sister, Ranelle, played the imaginary piano. My brother Bennoit would do the preaching. Sharron (my younger sister) and I would be the "audience." When it came time to baptize, my brother would take us into the tall weeds and duck us below the top of the weeds. Occasionally Bennoit would step over to one of us and pat us on the knee, and say, "Ain't that right brother, sister?"

Dad used to whip us pretty regularly when we needed it. Sometimes we would get it when we didn't need it!!! If we were all misbehaving he would grab the one closest to him (usually me) and spank that one. My back side has seen a variety of whipping weapons: hoe handle, cotton stalk, belt, razor strap, and his hand. We all lived though it and none were worse for the wear!

One house that we lived in had a trash dump close by. I liked to go over there and see what I could find. Once I found a little bottle of what I thought were redhots. They actually were Lydia A. Pinkham's pills (maybe kidney pills?). It is a good thing they tasted terrible for I spit them out right away.

Dennis liked to play in the little creek nearby catching crawdads. One day he was intrigued by a crawdad that looked a little different. Its tail curled up instead of lying flat. He took it home to mom on a flattened tin can. My mother almost had a heart attack. It was a scorpion.

Another pastime was to walk around on stilts. We would make the foot holds so high that we would have to climb up on a ladder or something tall to get them on our feet. Then we would bravely stomp around on the red ant beds. Those ants were quite large and would leave a welt when they bit.

My dad left Ft. Worth to go back to Quanah to establish Bible Baptist Church. We settled down in Quanah until my sophomore year of high school. It was here at Bible Baptist Church that the Lord gloriously saved me. (I was 11 years old, and I am sure my parents were getting concerned about me.) The Lord had me under conviction for several months. I had been used to going with my dad to pick up people for church. When the Lord began dealing with me, I didn't want to go with him anymore. I was afraid he would talk to me about being saved. The Lord used Lorene Null (wife of Fred Null – former missionary to the Philippines) to help bring conviction. I remember watching her powder her nose. She looked up at me and just asked me, "Winene, have you ever been saved?" That made me start to think seriously about my sins and need of salvation.

When I went forward one Sunday during the invitation my dad asked why I had come. I replied, "I want to be saved." We didn't pray a prayer and there was no lightning. Years later I wondered whether or not I had actually been saved – because we didn't pray. Finally I realized that salvation is all of God and none of me. It didn't even depend on a carefully worded prayer. He knew my heart and HE gloriously saved me.

Weekly we made trips to the laundromat to

wash our clothes. The washers were all ringer type with two or three tubs for washing and rinsing. I remember mother using something called "bluing" with the white clothes. It was supposed to make the whites whiter. It was a full day's work to get the clothes washed and back home to hang them on the clothesline. Sometimes one of us would be "helping" and would get our arm hung up in the ringer. Mom was very quick to hit the release before we lost a limb!!!

After dad entered the ministry we did all kinds of work to supplement our income. Our family hired out to local farmers doing cotton pulling in the fall and hoeing weeds in the cotton fields in the summer. I guess we were migrant workers before it became "cool" to be migrant workers. We had farmers lined up to keep us busy the entire summer. We knew each farmer and what kind of weeds we would have to deal with. One had careless weeds that were tough to chop down. Another had goat heads (sticker weeds) that formed a carpet and we had to find the roots and roll it back like a carpet. Another had Johnson grass whose roots penetrated to the middle of the earth. (Some farmers had us just cut it off even with the ground and others wanted it dug out as far as we could.) I remember going barefoot and hopping from cotton plant to cotton plant to keep my feet in the shade so they wouldn't burn. (We had shoes, but just hadn't wanted to wear them.) We had sun bonnets that we were supposed to wear; but did not like to wear them because of the heat. Mother said we were going to bake our brains!

One farmer came out to "help" us. His rows were quite lengthy, and; after a round or two he said to my dad, "Let's sit down and blow a spell." (Blow a spell means to rest a bit.) My dad told him to go ahead and cool down, but we would keep on working. At the time, I couldn't understand why he didn't want to do what the boss suggested! Another farmer had a field that had only scattered weeds. We children loved that field – but I remember my mother saying that it was just too much walking!!

A prank we used to play on mother was to get a dried devil's claw (a shriveled pod with very sharp, curled tendrils) and sneak up behind her and hook that devil's claw around her ankle. As we did this we would hiss like a snake. Never failed to get a good reaction!

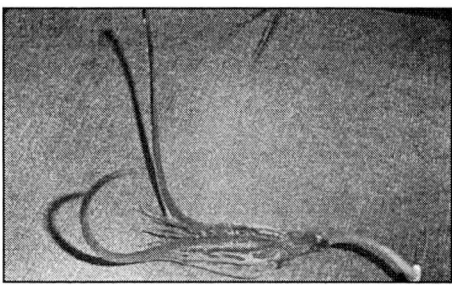

Devil's claw

In the fall of the year our school was dismissed for "cotton pulling" time. I would much rather have been in school!! Some of the fields were quite sandy and I remember being told to shake the sand out of the cotton that we picked up from the ground. I didn't shake mine very well because I knew it would weigh more with the sand. (We were paid by the pound.)

My sister, Ranelle, had a friend whose name was Texas Lacey. She was a very pretty raven-haired girl. When she happened to leave a capsule of hair dye behind on the sink, I decided it was time for me to see how I would look with black hair. There was not enough dye in that one capsule for my long tresses. It was several weeks before my green hair grew back to its natural color.

My first long trip away from home by myself came when I was a freshman in high school. My Aunt Myrtle Seitz took me with her to visit her daughter, Ernestene Patton, in Amarillo. That was about 140 miles. It seemed like a great distance to me. As we entered Amarillo (a very large city to me) the footfeed (accelerator to you) began to stick. My aunt had to put her foot underneath it and bring it back up. She was very nervous and I was scared to death. Luckily we got there okay; and probably Ernestene's husband, Leroy, fixed the problem.

At the middle of my sophomore year Dad decided to go to Springfield, Missouri and enroll in Baptist Bible College to finish his Bible training. How I hated Central High School in Springfield. I was accustomed to about 175 in our entire high school. The school in Springfield was quite large with 500 or more in the sophomore year alone. The lockers were a frustration for me. I didn't know how to work the combination lock. The campus was made up of several buildings and I was always getting lost. There was a linen delivery truck parked by the door I entered after my PE class. I was always so nervous that the truck would not be there at the time I needed it. At one point my schedule was changed and I went to my usual lunch period (there were 3 or 4 lunch periods). Afterwards I went to the biology class assigned to me. When I walked in, the class was in session. The stern faced teacher asked me what I was doing there. I told him I thought I was supposed to be in the class. Later when the class broke for their lunch period he locked me in the room. (This class was split in the middle for lunch.) I never did enjoy dissecting frogs, going to lunch, and coming back to finish the frog job.

I was accustomed to playing first chair, second clarinet in our high school band. In Springfield I was last chair, third clarinet (the very bottom spot).

It was a great thing for me if I could successfully hit one note out of each measure. Band surely wasn't much fun anymore.

At one point while we were living in Springfield, Sharron and I had a big fight. Mother and dad were gone for a little while. When they came home they found me locked in the bathroom and Sharron waiting outside the door with a brick. (It's a good thing I could run fast, or I might not be here today!) Needless to say, we were both in trouble!

I guess my dad missed pastoring. The following summer he accepted a pastorate in Eureka, Kansas. After pastoring there a short while he accepted pastorate of Faith Baptist Church in Attica, Kansas.

Attica was a very small town, which was much more to my liking. I graduated from high school in Attica after attending 4 different high schools in three different states. My credits got all messed up and I almost had to attend another year of high school. The school was small enough that I was moved back to first chair second clarinet, and even played in a clarinet quartet that won second place at the state competition. This made me feel better after my experience in Springfield.

## BIBLE COLLEGE (1956 – 1959)

The fall after graduation from high school found me enrolling in Baptist Bible College in Springfield.

(This was in the fall of 1956. BBC was much more conservative back then!)

My years at BBC were a joyous time of my life. It is true that I had no financial support and worked for 50 cents an hour doing housework and babysitting. Dorm rent was $13.00 a month plus I had to eat and buy books. The Lord marvelously supplied. Only once do I remember that I was hungry enough to eat a tablespoon of mayonnaise that my roommate had. (This was due to putting a dress on lay-away and not using my money wisely.) Mayonnaise does not set well on an empty stomach!!

There is much to be said about the fun we had in the girls' dormitory. We were always playing pranks – like the time I stood in our darkened room with my hand placed over the light switch waiting for my roommate, Norma Harms Bledsoe, to come in. The scream was worth the wait!

Jorene Mullens Howard and I had fun one Friday night when we were dateless. (Friday night was the only night dates were allowed). We hid in the bushes while other more fortunate girls were being escorted to the door from the parking lot. We knew the guy would return and would have to move his car to the boys' dorm parking lot. It was fun to sneak into the space between the seats and then as the guy was driving along, we would tap him on the shoulder or make some kind of noise. One fellow almost ran into the stone gate that was the entrance to their parking area. Another, Tom McGath, told me he was going to take me out and keep me out past the 11:00 curfew. (Which he did!!) It was not a problem because I had already notified Joyce Wallace Beggs whose job it was to watch the door for latecomers.

Two dorm rooms were situated with a shower between. Six girls shared one bathroom/shower. When taking a shower we usually left the doors unlocked in case of an emergency. What fun it was to reach in and turn the knob that would make the shower turn ice cold. We did not have air conditioning and I remember how hard it was to get into my clothes after a shower. The humidity was so bad that I felt the shower really did no good.

One time the girls in the dorm got me really good. I had been out and came back to my room to find a large box in the middle of the room with a jacket thrown on top of it. Of course, I wondered why the big box with a coat on top. As I lifted the coat someone jumped out of the box at me. I'm sure Mrs. Donnelson (dorm mother) could hear me scream!

On April 1 of our graduating year I had a lot of fun with Colleen Herber. At that time I was working in the college office. I told Colleen that we had been working on counting credits to make sure who would actually graduate. I told her that it looked like she needed another half credit to graduate. Of course, the registrar, Doris Gordon, was in on the prank. When Colleen went to ask her about the credit, Doris confirmed that she thought that was correct. Then she said, "Just let me count your credits one more time." She turned from the window and wrote on a piece of paper which she handed to Colleen. The paper actually said, "April Fool!!" Colleen returned to class with a beet red face. It's a good thing that class was getting under way or I might not be here today!!

Even with the fun, I did find time to study, work, go on street meetings, and teach a primary class at High Street Baptist Church.

Fred Nimmo and I met at BBC and started dating during our senior year. I was dating two guys at the time and eventually was being pressured to make a choice. Obviously my choice was Fred. Within a week's time of my announcing my decision, Fred came to me saying that he had a letter from an old girlfriend in California (Paris Arakelian) telling him that she was planning to come to Springfield for his graduation. What a dilemma!!

The other guy (Ronald Ballard) told me that he would be my escort for all the "Graduation Week" activities. (He even gave me a beautiful Bible as a graduation present – what a gracious fellow!) What a wonderful, miserable week that was! I kept trying to see how Fred was faring with his old girlfriend. Later I found out he was trying to assess the situation with me and my old boyfriend.

As we sang "God Be with You 'Til We Meet Again" after the final graduation night service my heart was heavy with thinking that I might never see Fred again! After graduation both "others" left for their respective states.

In the late summer Fred approached me and asked me out again. (He was pastoring Bible Baptist Church in Mt. Vernon, MO at the time.) I told our mutual friend, Eva Tomberlin, that I was not interested in casual dating. So she passed the word that I would accept a date with him only if he was interested in a serious relationship. By November or December we were engaged. He felt it was important for me to visit church with him in Mt. Vernon to announce our engagement. I didn't know at the time that there was in the church a widow's daughter who had eyes for him. They had invited him to dinner several times. Fred is naïve at times, and didn't pick up on it until a church member pointed it out.

## MARRIAGE AND EARLY MINISTRY

We were married on March 17, 1960, at High Street Baptist Church (Fred's home church) with my father, W. S. Herring, officiating. (Bro. W.E.

Dowell took part as my father gave me away.)

 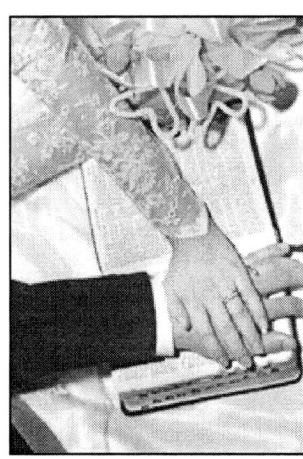

Dress made by Colleen Herber Rigsby

With Fred's "mustering out" pay from the Navy we honeymooned in Florida. What a wonderful time we had visiting his friends there. The Dinsbeers in Jacksonville were such gracious hosts. Fred was leader of their Youth Department just before coming to BBC. We went on board an aircraft carrier, ate fresh oranges and grapefruit from roadside stands, got our feet wet in the Atlantic near St. Augustine, enjoyed a glass-bottomed boat ride near Winter Haven, and visited a friend of Fred's from Springfield in Pensacola Beach.

Back in Mt. Vernon we rented a very small upstairs apartment. (Just a curtain separated the bed from the living room– not exactly a bedroom.)

We came to love and appreciate those people in Mt. Vernon. They were so good to us. I believe Fred received $25.00 a week salary. He also did mail delivery. We had a '53 Chevy which kept running out of gas because the gauge was broken. Fred would always write down the mileage and kept thinking he could get a few more miles out of the tank.

The first time I went out to the laundromat to wash clothes I ran over a culvert and ruined a tire. I cried and cried because I thought I had ruined the entire wheel. Fred comforted me and said not to worry, it could be fixed. The first chocolate pie I made turned out to be chocolate soup!!

Things moved pretty fast in our first year of married life. In August we took the young people to attend Sagmount Youth Camp near Joplin, MO. Little did we know that we would end up surrendering our lives to the mission field. (I would not encourage moving this quickly in your first year of marriage.)

### DEPUTATION

That fall we packed up what little we had and started deputation (visiting churches to raise support to go to Alaska.) We had been married a scant 6 months. Our slogan was "Nimmos to the Eskimos" and we used the verse on our prayer cards: Job 38:22 **"Has thou entered into the treasures of**

**the snow?…"** We even had our first prayer cards cut in the shape of an igloo.

First prayer card picture, 1960

We had some great blessings while visiting different churches all over the U.S. Later, I think missionaries tried to raise support in adjoining states so they would not have to drive so many miles. We just went wherever anyone would have us; and we pretty well covered the states. Some churches gave us large love offerings and some struggling churches did well to feed us lunch. I remember more than once Fred returned the offering to the pastor because he could see the financial struggles. We did not have a dime in the bank, but the LORD supplied all we needed.

Once we were provided a place to sleep in an apartment of Grace Baptist Church in downtown Oklahoma City. We were so very tired upon our arrival that we only took inside what we needed for the night. Everything else we had in the world was locked in our station wagon in the parking lot. The next morning Fred discovered that thieves had broken in and taken almost everything; clothes, records, clarinet, etc. His mother had hand quilted two beautiful crib quilts for our son. Of all the things taken those quilts were the most valuable to me. They were irreplaceable. She was no longer able to do any quilting. When my brother, Dennis Herring, heard about our episode he said, "I guess Fred was not so concerned about what he would preach on – but what he would preach in!"

A couple of months into deputation I began to feel nauseous in the mornings. You're right, I was pregnant. After consulting with the doctor we were told that I could travel as long as I was careful; but, near the end I would have to settle down for the delivery. One morning in Tennessee I remember having a breakfast of oatmeal with our host family. After excusing myself I lost everything in the bathroom, then came back to finish my breakfast. (I didn't want them to think the oatmeal had made me sick!)

The next week we were in Nashville in the morning service and Knoxville for the evening service (almost half way across the state!) I was so exhausted and relieved when the pastor told us we were booked into a motel. Across the bed I fell and just cried out my tears. I am so thankful for the many host families who took us in and fed us – but when you are pregnant and completely worn out, all you want is some alone time.

My mother had told us that as the time neared for delivery I could come and stay with them. Fred's mother had graciously made the same offer. So, with two alternatives, I thought what could go wrong?

Within the month previous to my delivery Fred's mother had heart surgery and my mother had a hysterectomy. There went my two choices.

### PAUL'S BIRTH

On May 10, 1961 we had a newborn son, Stanley Paul. He was named for Stan Flynn (missionary to Japan, and Paul DeMott (faithful deacon at Bible Baptist Church in Mt. Vernon.) As I looked at him in the nursery of the hospital I noticed how olive his complexion was – not pink like the other babies. I just thought that was pretty neat – until I learned that he was jaundiced. (I didn't even know what the word meant.)

A curious coincidence occurred at the hospital.

After I was placed in a room, I happened to see Louise Ballard in the hallway. She was enroute to the delivery room. I asked her to see if she could be placed in the room with me. (Remember her husband, Ronald, was the "other" beau during my senior year of college.) So, we ended up rooming together.

On the fourth day after delivery the doctor asked me if there was anything I wanted. He probably expected me to say I wanted to go home – but I didn't know where "home" was. I really didn't want to leave the safety of the hospital!

Our dear friends, Ron and Ruth Reeves, helped Fred locate a little furnished apartment to rent. I still don't know where they came up with dishes, linens, etc. Fred was there for about a week or two. He then left to visit more churches to raise support. Different friends from High Street Baptist Church and BBC came and spent the nights with me for awhile. It was there I found out how large Missouri cockroaches could get. Paul's crib was a tiny car bed propped up on two chairs in the living room.

As soon as I was strong enough we resumed traveling with Fred. As a result of this, I believe Paul was a very insecure baby. Once at a church in Kansas I was asked to leave him in the nursery. I told them that he would probably cry the whole time. They assured me he would be okay. I told them to send someone for me if they needed me. Not even half way through I was summoned to help. Later I was told that everyone had tried to comfort him, even the janitor! Another time at the pastor's house he had diarrhea that leaked all over their couch. Talk about being embarrassed!

### ON OUR WAY TO ALASKA

After saying our tearful goodbyes to my parents and the Fellowship Baptist Church in Spearman, Texas (where my dad was pastor), we worked our way north and west to Seattle, WA. In December of 1961 we flew out of Seattle on an old propjet on our way to Anchorage. I had not flown much prior to that trip. (Since then I have flown many, many miles on almost every aircraft available.) There was fire streaming out behind the engines. Not thinking that looked too good, I asked the stewardess if that was a common sight. She assured me that all was okay.

It took 6 hours or more to get to Anchorage from Seattle (a non-stop flight). As I looked down at the snow capped mountains I became concerned that there would be any place of habitation in that vast land of snow.

No one met us at the airport in Anchorage. We hired a taxi to a motel in downtown Anchorage. After about two weeks visiting with Bible Baptist Church in Anchorage, Fred felt led to drive up to

Fairbanks. (This was in the middle of January – not a very good time for that snowy, icy trip.) About 50 miles out of Anchorage we slid into a large berm of snow at the right side of the road. We knew we had to keep the engine going to keep us warm. Fortunately, someone came along and helped pull us out. (I was more than ready to return to Anchorage – but Fred was determined to go on to Fairbanks.) As we drove along I would notice "emergency shelters" by the side of the road. I would try to remember how far it was from one shelter to the next.

### FAIRBANKS

In Fairbanks the Allen Swires welcomed us into their home. We helped with the work at Bible Baptist Church where Bro. Swires was the missionary/pastor. Fred enrolled in some classes at the University of Alaska to learn more about the native people.

We rented a small one bedroom apartment for $155.00 a month. At that time we thought it was a lot of money compared to stateside prices.

Paul slept in his crib in the living room. As he was nearing a year old I decided he should be able to go to sleep by himself. After feeding him, rocking him, and making sure he had a dry diaper, I put him in his crib. He cried and cried and cried. Our neighbors came over to see if he was ill or if there was anything they could do. I was already about to pull my hair out; then I felt like pulling their hair out!!

More than once we left our cars running for the entire church service, so that they would not be frozen up afterwards. At that time there were no outdoor plug-ins located at the church for the widely used head bolt heaters.

As we prayed and looked at a map of Alaska we felt that the Lord would have us go to Bethel. We inquired and found that there had never been a Baptist Church in that vast southwestern area of Alaska. (We later learned that the denominations had been 'assigned' to certain areas of the state in the 1880's.) The Baptists were given the interior area around Anchorage, south central Alaska, and Kodiak; the Lutherans were assigned to the Nome area; Covenants were assigned the Unalakleet area; the Moravians were given the southwest area – including Bethel; the Friends were given the Kotzebue area; and the Episcopals were to minister to interior Alaska. Presbyterians were given the Barrow area (way up north). We didn't realize we were going out of the area assigned to Baptists!

## BETHEL (1962 – 1964)

Bethel is situated approximately 400 air miles west of Anchorage on the Kuskokwim River. This river is second in size to the mighty Yukon. Bethel is reached only by air or the river. The river is navigated by boats and float planes in the summer time and all sorts of vehicles in the winter time. When the river is solidly frozen it is used by cars, trucks, and airplanes. The Kuskokwim winds around like a snake and as you fly in to Bethel you circle the village. I mistakenly thought our Quonset faced the south – but later realized that the sun didn't set in the south!!

Aerial view of Bethel

    Small as it was, Bethel was the hub of commerce and fishing in the southwest area of Alaska. When we first arrived in Bethel there was approximately one mile of roads in the entire village. We did all of our visiting by walking.

Truck, planes on frozen Kuskokwim

In June Fred went ahead to find a place for us to live. He called back to me in Fairbanks saying that housing was very scarce. Any livable place was rented or reserved for school teachers. Finally he found a place. His description was that it looked like a chicken coop in the middle of a junk yard. When I arrived I realized that he was not exaggerating. There were windows across one side that faced a fish drying rack. Every morning we would awake to kill all the flies that had come in during the night. We decided to count them. I can't remember the count; but it was a huge amount. We debated sending them in an envelope to one of our supporting pastors – but thought better of it.

In later years we visited Bethel and saw lots of improvements since the time we were there. They have since built a regional high school. Much of the village now has running water and indoor plumbing.

Chicken coop in Bethel, our first house

Our Quonset mansion

We had no running water or bathroom facilities. (This was before disposable diapers were in common use. Therefore, I washed dirty diapers in Brown Slough nearby). The bed was a little larger than a twin size. I don't know what the mattress was made of – but it was lower on one side than the other, and lumpy. Whoever was on the high side always rolled down on the other one during the night! We heated water in a skillet on the small oil stove. Fred said that was the first time he took a "skillet bath"!

We were advised to find better living quarters before winter set in. We were told that the people who lived there before could see their breath between them over the oil stove in the winter time.

One of the first families we met came to visit us in that little shack. We asked the Ashepaks how many children they had. The man counted up and said he had five children. Then he remembered the child they had given to his sister which made six. (The sister was not able to have children.) This was shocking news to us.

Fortunately, we found there was a Quonset hut for sale by some school teachers. We speedily made the deal and moved in during the month of October. Our wringer washing machine was put in a boat in the slough nearby and barged down a short way to the Kuskokwim River. The Quonset was on the shore of the river. After living in the little chicken coop, the Quonset hut looked like a mansion.

Neighborhood children, our jeep

Fanny & Eliza Jacobs; their dad, George, built our little boat

Supply ship from Seattle

There were a couple of small grocery stores, but groceries were very expensive because most of them were flown out from Anchorage. Mrs. Bob Leight in Nome helped me figure out how to contact a company in Seattle to have our order shipped from there to Bethel in the summer. (We had 3 ships from Seattle in the summer time). When that huge boat arrived and blew the foghorn everyone in the village headed to the dock in front of the village. It didn't matter if it was midnight or 3:00 a.m. There would be all sorts of goodies arriving; even cars, and once, a mobile home. It was hard to estimate how much we would need of certain items to last us a year.

Early church service in Bethel. Adolf and Maggie Lind in the back row.

There was a little shed beside the Quonset where we began having services. After awhile it became pretty crowded – but was a good beginning. On one occasion when Paul was misbehaving in church, I decided to take him out for a little pat on the behind. One little boy followed me all the way saying, "Mrs. Nimmo, he be good, Mrs. Nimmo he be good!" It was hard to correct him with that little lad pleading for him.

Paul in his "parky" in Bethel

Another time several children came in to play with Paul and Ron. My heart sank as I noticed the big sores of impetigo on their faces and lips. They were loving and kissing on Paul and Ron. After they left, I thoroughly washed Paul's and Ron's faces and mouths with soap and water. They probably wondered if I had gone crazy. (They never did come down with impetigo.)

Paul was just a little over a year old and learning to walk. Have you ever tried to walk on tundra? In the summer time it thaws underneath and becomes like clumps of sponges so that there is a spring in almost every step you take. Imagine trying to learn to walk on that!

Bethel is positioned on permafrost. This means that areas of the ground underneath remain frozen year round. When Fred tried to put up a clothes line for me it took him three days. He had to dig until he hit frozen soil, pour in hot water and wait for that to thaw before digging again.

A new grade school was being built. Electrical lines were run along the water pipes and foundation. In the winter time they kept the water from freezing and in the summer time they kept the foundation from thawing. (Many of the houses in Bethel were not level because of the thawing in the summer time.)

One of our first converts (and I mean that literally -- our convert) was John, the Baptist. We thought how neat it was that the first one saved had the name of Baptist attached to his name. Then we found out that the next day he and his friend had gotten very drunk. (We later found that the Eskimo people were very gracious and agreeable. We had to be careful not to talk them into a profession of faith that was only to please us.)

## THE LANGUAGE - YUPIK

Soon after our arrival in Bethel we endeavored to learn the Yupik language. Many of the Eskimos were bilingual – but the older and very young spoke only Yupik. While we could have gotten by without learning the language, we felt strongly that it was best to learn their language. We learned many single words and the names of things – but were at a loss as to how to form a sentence. Those native people trying to help us did not know how to show us either. We are grateful to our dear friend, Maggie Lind, for helping work on the language through many long hours.

Soon an opportunity arose for Fred to fly back to Fairbanks for an intensive course in Yupik. A linguist, Irene Reed, had just been commissioned by the university to put the Yupik language on paper. She agreed to tutor Fred for three months. This was a once in a lifetime opportunity. Moravian missionaries mastered the Yupik language in the late 1800's and early 1900's. They translated the New Testament and many hymns. (We purchased and used their hymnals in our services.) However, their spelling was not linguistically correct. They used a German type spelling.

Fred worked very hard on learning the language. Before long he was able to read some of the Bible and bring part of his messages in Yupik. We sang all of our songs in Yupik. I remember one service where a very young Eskimo girl sat up and pointed her finger right at Fred and said, "Gussek!" She was amazed that the Gussek (native word for white man) was speaking her language.

Fred was always working on learning new words. He was given the name "IgaRta" which means "the writer". (He carried pen and paper to write down any new words or phrases.) He translated some songs and the tract, God's Simple Plan of Salvation. I believe he gained much respect for his effort to learn the language. The other missionaries at that time did not learn the language, but depended on the Eskimos' understanding of English. This worked okay for words taken literally. But, as we know, so much of the Bible is spiritual in meaning and contains many intangibles.

One evening three older Eskimo women got brave enough to visit in our home. They understood very little English and we understood very little Yupik. We struggled to communicate. After a while I could see that they were getting antsy and acting as if they wanted to leave, but just didn't know how to excuse themselves. I came up with the idea of trying to tell them "Good night" in Yupik. The phrase I should have used was "unuuq asiliria." Instead I said, "Aanaq asiliria", which actually meant good excrement. Those three women were surely snickering as they left. Only later did I find out from Maggie Lind what I had said.

## VILLAGE LIFE

On another occasion my friend, Nellie Forbes, stood up in service, loosened a belt that held her baby in place on her back, and began wiggling until the baby slipped out on the chair behind her. Fred was really worried about what was going on before he saw the baby drop on the seat. Nellie and I had many fun experiences.

Nellie was a native from Shishmaref and married to Bill, who worked for the local airlines. Because of this, they were better off financially than most of the native people. They had a boat with an inboard motor.

One day Nellie and I decided we would take her husband's boat out. It was tied up in Brown Slough which flowed into the mighty Kuskokwim. Neither she nor I had ever handled an inboard that was guided by a steering wheel. You should have seen us dodging boats and float planes that were anchored along the slough as she over corrected from one side to the other. Finally we were in the middle of the river when a boat came speeding directly into our path. Nellie didn't know how to slow us down. The other boat barely missed us.

Nellie Forbes, Sophie Moses (Peggy's mother), and Mrs. Anaruk. Notice embankment down to the river. Quonset was just to the right of the boardwalk.

Most of the boats were open skiffs handmade by the Eskimos. We had a sturdy little boat made by Mr. Jacobs, about 17 feet long. We used it to visit nearby villages and fish camps on the other side of the river. Once when we decided to visit the fish camps, there were great waves on the river. Even the Eskimos were not out in their boats! In the middle of the river Fred decided we should turn back. I thought for sure we were going to end up in the brink while trying to turn around in the middle of the giant waves. I know our Heavenly Father was surely watching over us that day.

Adolf and Maggie Lind's fish drying rack

Another day as we neared the slough where we always anchored our boat, Fred told me to get back by the motor and guide it in. He would get up in the bow and be ready to jump out with the anchor. I told him I did not know how to do it. He had more confidence than I did. As we neared the shore, instead of slowing the motor, I revved it up (having turned the handle the wrong way.) Fred ended up in the bushes. I don't think he ever asked me to do that again!

In the fish camps the available food was asaliaq and meqtuq. Asaliaq was a fried pancake that bubbled up in the pan. It was really quite tasty. Meqtuq was dried fish strips. They had quite an odor – but we learned to like it very much.

Another delicacy was akutaq, or Eskimo ice cream. It consisted of wild berries, seal oil, and sugar. Our first experience of trying akutaq was in a fish camp. The seal oil had become rancid. Needless to say we hardly got it down. Later we were introduced to akutaq made with Crisco and it was really quite good.

The Eskimos have a tradition that requires them to share some of their first catch of fish. Only then will they have a successful fishing season. Due to this tradition we were kept loaded with wonderful salmon to eat without having to fish at all ourselves. The largest fish ever given to us was a 55 pounder – a king salmon. (This is not a fish story – here is the picture to prove it!) The steaks cut from that fish were so large they would hardly fit on a large dinner plate.

Water truck in Bethel

As I mentioned before, we did not have running water. Instead we had two 55 gallon drums, one in the kitchen area and the other was for washing clothes. The village had one well that serviced the entire village. A large truck with a big wooden barrel on the back delivered water weekly. The large canvas hose was rolled out from the truck and across the living room floor. What a mess it made when it was muddy outside. One time as I was dipping water from the barrel I noticed big globs of black car grease in the water. I called the water man and he told me they had been working on the truck. His comment was, "I told those guys to run one or two barrels through before delivering water. I guess they didn't!"

Fred rigged up a gravity-flow shower. We would heat water on the oil stove, pour it into a small elevated barrel. He used some copper tubing to bring it down to a shower head. Another wire formed a circle to which we attached a shower curtain. A round metal bath tub was placed beneath it. The trick was to get the shower done before the tub got too full or too heavy to carry out and dump it out on the river bank.

Weekly washing of diapers was a must, especially after the Lord blessed us with another son. (More about Ron's birth a little later.) There was a huge diaper pail placed in our honey bucket room (to be explained later). There they would freeze. We would heat the water so that it was extremely hot. By the time the frozen diapers were thrown in the water temperature was about right. There were two clotheslines running down the middle of the living room/kitchen. We ducked diapers most of the time during the winter. The condensation from the wet diapers caused 2 feet of ice to form (vertically) on the inside of our walls.

Now for the honey bucket story. Our Quonset had a little room with a trap door leading to the outside. It was the honey bucket room. A truck (when it was running) would come and dump our bucket without ever entering the house. This was a pretty good arrangement when the truck was operative. Alas, about 25% of time the truck was broken down. Then we had the dilemma of how to dispose of the bucket's contents. Fred came up with the idea of climbing down the river bank (about 12 ft.), digging a hole, and burying it there. Then came the day when he slipped as he was carrying the bucket down. He came back in the house with a dented bucket in one hand and a pained expression on his face, asking, "Where's the Pine Sol?" I wanted to laugh so badly, but I knew by his expression that I had better not. It was years before he could laugh about what happened.

Finally the time came when we both got a big laugh out of it. When we were on furlough we were visiting a church down in Texas. Texas preachers can be very expressive at times. The speaker was telling about a meeting in which he had gotten a blessing from the messages and singing. His statement was: "Man it was so good; it was just like somebody had kicked over the honey bucket!" I looked at Fred and he looked at me. We really had to control ourselves to keep from bursting out laughing. The pew was shaking for quite a while.

There was a lake in the middle of the village called "Honey Bucket Lake." It was on this lake that I learned to ice skate. As I was skating along the children would warn me to avoid the small frozen mounds along the edge of the lake. Only later (during the spring thaw) did I learn that they were the frozen contents of honey buckets – hence, the name Honey Bucket Lake! That was an area to be avoided in the hot summer time. It was quite smelly!

Our house was heated by oil and we did our cooking on an oil stove. The fire box was at the side of the oven. I learned that when baking a cake I would have to turn it around mid way through or the cake would be lopsided. The stove top cooking was pretty slow. Some times when I would get in a hurry, I would remove the round lid and set the pot directly over the flame. The result was soot caked on the bottom of the pan – but I didn't care.

When it came time to clean this cook stove I was trying to bring the soot up through the firebox. As I was nearly finished an old Eskimo man named Otto came over and pulled out the drawer underneath exposing the place where most of the soot could be easily removed. Did I ever feel like a dumb Gussek!

One time a fellow came by our house and said he needed to borrow money for fuel oil. I think it was $20.00 that he needed. Fred lent him the money because the weather was quite cold. Within a month's time the same man stopped by. He needed $40.00 this time. He told us that with $20.00 of the $40.00 he would repay us the original $20.00 we had lent him! Sounds like a good deal to me!!

Maggie came by one day with two friends. They

were colorfully dressed and I asked them for a picture. They did not want to let me take a picture. (Some of them believe they will lose their shadow or spirit if they allow their picture taken.) After Maggie talked with them, they gave their assent. Later I asked Maggie how she got them to agree. She said, "I told them I would not interpret for them when they went to talk with some official if they didn't let you take a picture of them."

Women who didn't want picture taken

One evening Maggie was interpreting for a village meeting. The next day she came by to ask me about something the speaker had said. She said that he was not talking about hunting or anything along those lines when all of a sudden he said he had killed two birds with one stone. She said, "I interpreted it just as he said it, but I surely don't know what he meant."

Maggie helped us in so many ways. Someone had donated a full length mouton coat for my use when we got to Alaska. Maggie took one look at it and said, "Those sleeves are way too large, the lapel is too big, and you need a zipper and a hood." She took the fur from the sleeves and lapel and fashioned a hood, then put a ruff on the hood; and voila!, I had a very warm parka!!

Paul and me in my mouton parka made by Maggie Lind

Our sons used to call Maggie Maureluq Maggie; which means Grandma Maggie. They really loved her and she was so kind and friendly to them.

Maggie told me a "fish story". I still am not sure whether it was true or just her way of teasing me. She said that she had been ice fishing upriver and didn't get much fish; but she had lost her favorite lure.

Then about two weeks later she was ice fishing near Bethel (downriver). She caught a fish, and there was her lure that she had lost two weeks before.

### SMALL PLANE BUSH FLYING

We did quite a lot of flying by small plane. Our missionary friend, Dan Baldwin, flew us many miles. It was so smooth to land with floats on the river. However, not all of our flying went smoothly. On one occasion we were in Emongak on the lower Yukon when the exhaust line blew out. There are no repair shops of any kind in the smaller villages. Dan finally located an aluminum band to tighten around the line, hoping it would hold until we could get back to Bethel. We really prayed that the temporary fix would hold. God's Word says in Deuteronomy 33:27, **"The eternal God *is thy* refuge, and underneath *are* the everlasting arms…"** How I clung to that promise. We did make it back without any further mishap. God is so good!

Float plane flying was fun

Another time I was being flown out of Russian Mission. (I had been visiting a lonely, discouraged missionary wife there.) There was no airport, just a landing strip. There had been lots of rain and we were ankle deep in mud as we clambered aboard the Taylor Craft. The pilot said to me, "See that log about half way down the strip? If we are in the air by that time, we will make it." Bush flying will surely keep your prayer life current!! Amen!

Another missionary friend, Jim Jenkins, was making his first cross-country flight from Bethel to Anchorage in a Cessna 172. On board with him was a nurse, Fred, our two sons, and me. We had landed in Iliamna to refuel. We were about an hour out when the turbulence became rather bad. Jim decided he should return to Iliamna. As he headed back he could not locate the lights of the runway. The rest of those aboard could see them – but he couldn't see them. What a relief when our pilot finally saw the lights.

Another small plane flight is memorable to me. Those in the plane were Dan Baldwin (the pilot); John Sleppy; his son, Jody; my husband; and me. We were flying to Anchorage. This flight took several hours. Just before departure John told his son, Jody, to be sure and go to the bathroom. This I believe he did. Nevertheless, when we were in the air about an hour out of Bethel, Jody began to complain of his need to go to the bathroom. Alas, there were no facilities – no cans, no plastic bags. Dan remembered there was a military installation where we might be able to land. He could not raise them by radio. He decided to radio back to Bethel and see if they could contact the military installation. (No one can land at a military installation without express permission.) Bethel was able to contact them and we were given permission to land. Somehow the message regarding the emergency got mixed up. When we landed we were met with an ambulance and fire truck!! Leave it to the military to over react. It was well known that this airstrip made for a difficult landing and takeoff. It was situated between two mountains; so one had to come down rather abruptly and endeavor to get enough altitude to clear the mountain on the other side!

Commercial flying was interesting as well. On one flight returning from Anchorage to Bethel, we made three passes at the runway before the pilot decided he could not see the runway. We flew to McGrath and waited two or three hours until the fog lifted in Bethel. All flights into Bethel at that time were done with VFR (visual flight rules.)

## RON'S BIRTH

When I found out I was pregnant, I realized there were two options open to me for the birth of this second child. I could have the baby in Bethel at the doctor's house or I could fly in to Anchorage and have the baby at a hospital there. At the time Bethel had a Native Hospital, but I would not have qualified for care there. My choice was to stay in Bethel. Because I was due in January I did not like the thought of flying to Anchorage, and then back out to Bethel with a newborn. Usually the propjet landed in Dillingham to take on cargo. The cargo was not stowed beneath. The side of the plane opened up and the cargo was loaded next to our seats. The weather was frigid and the cold blast came right into the cabin during the loading process.

In December I awoke early one morning with pains that were exactly 5 minutes apart. I awakened Fred and told him. His response was, "Oh, it's too early you can't be in labor, go back to sleep." Which is exactly what he did!! Fortunately after awhile they subsided.

We did not have a car at the time. There were only a few private vehicles in the village. There were two friends who had told me to give them a call when I needed to go to the doctor.

I went into serious labor about 5:00 a.m. Sunday morning on January 19. I called the doctor and told her I would be there as soon as I could arrange a ride. The first volunteer was called with no answer. Then, I tried the second person with the same results. Then we tried the local cab company. Saturday night was a very busy night for them; therefore, no one answered their phone either. We were beginning to get concerned when the doctor called us back. She informed us that they had two vehicles, and if they could get one of them started her husband would come and get us.

My husband stayed behind to get Paul ready to take to another friend while I was at the doctor's house. He wrapped him up good and carried him to the friend's house. He told me that he had cried all the way. (Later the friend told me that he had wet his clothes, and they were frozen when he got there.) It was only 32 degrees below zero!

The doctor did not have running water in her house either. (The only place with running water was the Native Hospital.) It is rather difficult to be hygienic without running water. But I did the best I could. The doctor also had a baby about a year old. Although I was in pain that first night I did not want to ring the bell and disturb her because I could hear her baby crying into the night and knew she must be weary.

Ron in front of Dr. Schirmer's house in Bethel where he was born

We had a little bassinet for Ron. He was named Ronald Alan -- Ronald for our good friend, Ron Reeves; and Alan for Robert Allan Woosley, missionary in the Philippines. We kept his bassinet very near the oil heating stove to keep him warm. We thought it would be more convenient and best for me to breast feed him. This was done for about two months. He was still feeding about every two hours, so I thought my milk was not satisfying him. No one encouraged me or gave me any information on breast feeding – so I started giving him bottles. As I look back, I wish I had "hung in there" a little longer and breast fed him for a longer period of time. He was a good baby and we had many visitors because of having a newborn baby.

When Ron was about 2 weeks old, I resumed teaching the only Sunday School class that we had at the time. We met in our Quonset which was located next to the church. This class was composed literally of everyone who was not considered adult. The age range was from 2 weeks to about 14 years of age. What a challenge that was.

There was a church in Tucson, Temple Baptist Church. Their primary age department "adopted" Paul and Ron as their own "missionaries." They were so good to send everything imaginable for Christmas and their birthdays. Lesson ideas were also sent, which I adapted for use with the native children.

Let me digress just to say that we had a great number of churches who faithfully supported us. We were thankful for them. Because of them we did not need to worry about financial problems. It reminded me of the Scripture passage, II Corinthians 9:7&8 which says, **"Every man according as he purposeth in his heart,** *so let him give;* **not grudgingly, or of necessity: for God loveth a cheerful giver. And God** *is* **able to make all grace abound toward you; that ye, always having all sufficiency in all** *things,* **may abound to every good work:"**

Another Scripture that reminds me of Fred's attitude: II Corinthians 10:15-17, **"Not boasting of things without** *our* **measure,** *that is,* **of other men's labours; but having hope, when your faith is increased, that we shall be enlarged by you according to our rule abundantly, To preach the gospel in the** *regions* **beyond you,** *and* **not to boast in another man's line of things made ready to our hand. But he that glorieth, let him glory in the Lord."**

## MORE VILLAGE LIFE

Another friend was Maggie Michaels. I would visit her every week or so. When she became pregnant she complained of a lot of nausea. I told her to mention it to the doctor on her next visit. The next time I went to see her I asked her about the morning sickness and what the doctor had told her. She said, "Oh, he had me get some pills. Here is the bottle. It says to take in the mornings for nausea. I don't know what that word "nausea" means and I haven't taken any of them."

Another time I visited her, the house was rather odorific. She said, "Oh, you caught me at the wrong time. We were just having stinkheads." Stinkheads were made by digging a hole in the ground and burying the fish heads for about two weeks. Then they were dug up and eaten. We were never offered stinkheads. For this I am grateful, because I don't think I could have gotten it down. (We did try almost everything else that they had to offer.)

I was determined to try some seal meat which was given to us. The method most commonly used was to boil it. Well, I boiled it forever and ever. It was still so tough that we couldn't eat it. Another time when visiting, I was offered salmon which had been soaked in salt brine. As I was trying to eat it, the young son stood in front of me and ate an eyeball that was dangling from a piece of skin. I think he was mischievous and did that just to see how I would react!!

Katie Hales was a very old Eskimo woman originally from Nome. She was a baby when there was a grievous diphtheria epidemic in the village.

She told me that her only way of survival was for her to be put to nurse on a female dog. All the women of childbearing age had died. She told me about a time when she was walking alone at night and heard someone behind her. She became frightened and started running. Her expression was that her knees were water.

Chrissie Shantz, whose husband worked for the National Guard was fortunate enough to have a propane cook stove. The other women of the village were praising her for her bravery of cooking with gas. Maggie Lind relayed this story to me. She said that Chrissie would get her baking all ready to go in the oven. Then, she would invite a friend over for tea. While she had company she would do her baking so she wouldn't have to do it by herself! She was afraid of that gas stove!

Swansons' Store was in the middle of the village. During the summer they had a sale on canned goods by the case. By that time we had bought a little old jeep that was a reject from the Air Force (about '45 or '46 model). It was open air and good for summer time. I drove over to buy some canned goods. This sale was being held on the schoolyard. In the middle of this yard was the flagpole. Every July 4th this pole was greased and a $5.00 bill fastened to the top. (This was a big attraction for the celebration attended by many villages located along the Kuskokwim.) As

I left the sale I was thinking that I had the entire schoolyard in which to maneuver. As I put it in reverse there was a sharp jolt and a great cracking noise. Alas, I had knocked down the only flagpole in the village.

Another time as I was driving along at the fast pace of about 15 mph, I offered a ride to an older Eskimo woman. She gingerly got on board. As we drove along she grabbed the seat and kept saying, "Alingua, alingua!! That meant that she was afraid. When I asked her why she was afraid, she said it was her first time to ride in a car. Many of the native people flew in planes before they ever rode in a car!

We did not go to Alaska because of the great hunting and fishing. We went to minister to the Eskimo people. Fred was a city dude and had never done much hunting or fishing. One evening several men were telling their big fish stories. I shared with them that Fred was the best fisherman of them all because he had caught a 107 pound herring on dry ground in Missouri. They were all amazed that a herring could grow that large! (My maiden name was Herring).

The following poem that I wrote expresses my thoughts regarding Alaska:

## ALASKA CALLS

*Alaska, Alaska, what doth call me to you?*
*Is it your snow capped mountains, or your sky so blue?*
*Or the abundance of fresh air you so freely give?*
*That beckons, entices me here to live?*
*Or perchance it's the things I've heard in the lower 48*
*About this great, big, wonderful state.*

*Nay, nay, Alaska, 'tis none of these.*
*It's something far more important, if you please.*
*For all your beauty, you have no soul –*
*No pliable character which needs a good mold –*
*No decisions will you ever make –*
*You have no heart that might needlessly break.*

*'Tis your own dear people that beckon and call.*
*For their precious souls Christ gave his all.*
*This message of hope and help would I bring;*
*So they may share the song that I sing –*
*A song of Salvation and JOY unsurpassed,*
*A song unending that forever will last.*

One evening we decided to visit the Native Hospital. It was situated back on the tundra about a mile from the village. As we started home I looked at Fred and the mosquitoes were just swarming around his head. I mentioned this to him and he told me they were swarming around my head as well. We both started running – but to no avail. We were glad to finally get home and inside.

On another occasion we were invited for dinner by one of the nurses. She had an apartment within the hospital complex. As we were eating our dinner I suddenly heard a large surge of water. I said to Fred, "Oh my goodness, it is starting to pour rain. We must be getting home." What a laugh everyone had when they told us it was only the flush of the commode. I had not heard a commode flush in over a year.

One nurse had been told that when she came to Bethel she would need a year's supply of commodities. She had purchased a barrel of butter not knowing that she would have no place to store it. It started to become rancid. She asked us if we would like to have it. We got so accustomed to the taste of the rancid butter that when the supply was exhausted the other butter tasted rather flat!

Bethel had some pretty good rain storms in the fall. Our Quonset was on the bank of the Kuskokwim. It was a 12 – 14 feet drop down to the beach. There was already a great deal of erosion about 3 to 5 feet from our front door. During one of those storms the bank began to crack and crumble farther so that we began to be greatly concerned whether our house would end up falling down the river bank. Some men came and jacked up the Quonset and put it on huge timbers to make a sled. It was decided that if the bank held it would be easier to skid the house to another location after snow had fallen. "Thou wilt keep him in perfect peace whose mind is stayed on Thee."

The bank held and later after the snow had fallen the Quonset was moved quite a distance away from the river bank. It is now located in the heart of the village because others had to move as well.

After that storm we were in a boat on the river and could see many coffins sliding down the bank and into the river. Later some men tried to save as many as possible and moved the cemetery to a safer location. (When people died in the winter time their bodies were frozen for burial in the spring.)

Because of the tundra and permafrost there were no trees in Bethel. There was one tree and it was jokingly called "Bethel National Forest." The native people said there used to be trees, but they had been cut down for firewood.

After we were settled in I decided to start a Good News Club for the children. We lived very near the grade school. On Thursdays I would walk to the corner of the schoolyard and the children would know it was the day for GNC. One day a little girl approached me and said, "Can Catholics go to your GNC?" I said, "Of course, anyone can come to the GNC." Then she told me that the priest had told them that if they came to the GNC they could no longer go to his place to read funny books and play games. Then she said, "I'm coming anyway!" I think the priest created curiosity among the children, so that more of them came!

One little girl, Peggy Moses, came quite regularly. Sometimes her mother was not happy that she was coming. (More about this young girl later in the story.)

Good News Club in Bethel (Bro.
Bob Leight and Fred at back)
Peggy Moses is just below them in a
scarf
Diane Baxter is in second row from
bottom also in a scarf

We were living in Bethel when the great Alaskan earthquake occurred. Even though we were 400 air miles from Anchorage, we felt it. I was giving Ron his bottle. I began weaving back and forth. Never having experienced an earthquake, I thought I was getting sick. I was afraid that I would drop him – so I thought I would go outside for some fresh air. On second thought, it might be something in the atmosphere. If that is the case, I'd better get back inside and close the door. It was quite a while before we learned what had happened. We only had one radio station beamed by the Armed Forces. It was off the air for most of the day.

A few days later our friend related this story. He thought he was getting sick – so went to wash his face. He grabbed a towel that the children had used. It happened to have some mud on it. When he looked in the mirror and saw his streaked face he thought he really was sick. He headed for the doctor's office. Only then did the doctor tell him what had happened.

At one time we had an Eskimo girl (Lucy Nakowallera) who was pregnant stay with us. She was from a nearby village, Napakiak, and wanted to be close to the hospital for delivery. At the time we had run out of sugar. As I gave her a cup of tea I offered her saccharin to sweeten it. She refused to put any of those little pills into her tea! (Maybe she thought I was trying to poison her!)

Later her mother came by for a visit. We were having a snack and I asked her to join us. I had just put bread in the toaster. You should have seen her eyes grow big and she nearly jumped out of her seat when that bread ejected! Guess she had never seen a toaster.

Our neighbors were the Baxters. There were two children, Diane and Billy. Diane was a very sweet girl. She made a profession of faith. That same year she began dragging her foot a little. When she was taken to the doctor he sent her to Anchorage for further valuation. She was diagnosed with a brain tumor. I think she lived 6 months to a year afterward. She assured us that she was not afraid of death and was a good witness for the Lord.

Her mother was "Bunny." This name came from the Yupik word Panik (pa-neek), which means daughter. In Yupik the letters "B" and "P" sound very similar. So, Panik was shortened to "Bunny." She took me with her to check her ptarmigan snares. She had no birds in her snares, but I had an experience I will not forget. I kept sinking down in the snow up to my armpits. By the time we got home I was exhausted. I never offered to go with her again!!

We had lots of blueberries growing in the field behind our Quonset (after it was moved from the river bank.) One day Nellie Forbes and her children

were visiting. Paul, with one of her girls (Rachel)
and Billy, decided to pick blueberries. After a while
they returned to the house. Rachel had a container
quite full of blueberries. Paul had very few berries –
but he did have quite blue lips!!

Rachel and Billy Forbes and Paul picking blueberries

### KAKO YOUTH CAMP

We had Youth Camps up on the Lower Yukon
River. These Youth Camps were started by John and
JoAn Sleppy who organized the camp and facilitated
getting the children to the site. They went to a lot of
work and expense. Only eternity will reveal the good
done in the lives of many Eskimo children. They
would be flown from Bethel to Russian Mission by
Dan Baldwin. From Russian Mission they would go
by boat to the site (a former trapper's cabin on the
Yukon River).

Study time in meeting hall made from logs and plastic
Fred in plaid shirt at left, John Sleppy on right (with glasses)

It was tent city. There were no facilities at all. When going to the outhouse we would first light up the Buhach (a powdered insect repellant). Then after the resident mosquitoes were dead, we could proceed. Fred used a mosquito net because he reacted badly to mosquito bites.

We had one week of younger children, followed by a week with the older children. Another worker and I decided we would go over behind a little island and wash up in the river. Upon returning to the camp, I was about ready to step out of the boat. She decided to follow me. The weight of two of us on the same side of the boat caused it to capsize. Into the muddy brink we went. (So much for getting cleaned up!!) The children headed quickly to their tents to get their cameras. They all had a big laugh. The kids liked to swim in the Yukon River. It was so cool it would take your breath away.

We always kept a smudge fire going to keep the mosquito population down. The Eskimo kids would go fishing almost every day. A favorite of theirs was roasted fish hearts. The taste wasn't so bad; but it was hard to see them still beating as they were thrust into the fire!

Fred and Ron at Youth Camp
Fred in mosquito netting

## BACK TO BETHEL

It was spring time and time for the smelts (hooligans) to run. The native people love to fry up a pan of them. Fred visited a family and was asked to share the smelts with them. Unfortunately these small fish feed in the slough. The slough is used by many to dump their honey buckets. This caused an epidemic of hepatitis in the village. Fred began to feel lethargic and his urine turned to a rusty, orange color. We were planning a trip to Anchorage anyway. Upon examination by a doctor in Anchorage he was hospitalized with hepatitis and placed in isolation for 18 days.

When he began to feel better, it was decided that I should return to Bethel. It was then that Peggy (remember her from GNC?) asked if she might stay with me to help keep me company.

One night when we had finished devotions, she said to me, "Will you please show me how to be saved?" Gladly I went though the Scriptures and she prayed for salvation. The next day she asked, "Do you have a pencil and paper? I want to write to your husband in the Anchorage hospital and tell him. (I still have the letter. It is a treasure to me). At this writing Peggy is a grandmother. Doesn't seem possible. She has a daughter, two sons, and several grandchildren who are not saved. We correspond occasionally by E-mail and telephone.

When Fred was released from the hospital he was told to do absolutely nothing for six months. We decided it would be best to take a furlough for his recuperation.

## FIRST FURLOUGH

My dad was pastoring Fellowship Baptist Church in Spearman, Texas. We decided to rent a small apartment in Spearman for Fred's recuperation. Mother helped me a lot with Paul and Ron. The apartment had no laundry facilities. Many days I spent visiting with mom and getting the wash done. We enjoyed and appreciated the people of Fellowship Baptist Church.

When Fred was better, we moved to Springfield, MO, to a little house owned by Dr. Donnelson (Missions Director of BBF). It was located just behind Baptist Bible College.

I remember Joan Weams Rohr once saying, "Furlough means that he is fur and I am low!!" That was surely true.

B.D. (as Bennoit was later called) decided to return to BBC for his 4th year. It was decided that it would be good for him to live with us because Fred would be traveling a lot on deputation. There was a basement room that fit the bill for him.

At this time my brother, Dennis (with his wife, Lois), were missionaries in Ethiopia. We received a letter from Dennis that he had heard that B.D. was dating a woman with two little boys. We got a big laugh out of that because we knew it was me with Paul and Ron. We never really figured out how that rumor got started. (We did attend High Street

Baptist Church together) and were probably seen together quite often!

Fred planned a trip up to the northeastern states. I had never seen that part of the country. We decided to see if mom and dad would come and stay with the boys so that I could travel with him for a few weeks. It was a great trip. I remember thinking that upstate New York reminded me so much of Alaska. We got to see Niagara Falls and made a night trip down into New York City. That's when I definitely decided I am a country girl. I remember praying that if the Lord would get us safely out of the city, I would never go there again. That's a promise I have kept! We were with Fred's cousin. We got lost several times and ended up in the black section of the city. We could not find the right bridge to get us back to Connecticut where he lived. We finally found it and then, someone tried to run us into the guard rail.

Our neighbors, in Springfield, were another missionary family. One day Mrs. Williams came over to ask me if I could take her to the vet to pick up her cat. I gladly agreed to do that because her husband was out on deputation as well. All went well until on the way home. Her cat got excited or scared and urinated all over her and the seat of the car. Our car was a new little Ford Falcon in a prairie gold color. I think it might have been our first new car. Unfortunately we were never able to get the smell out of that car. We tried everything possible. Finally, in desperation, we traded cars.

It was great living in Springfield because we could see all the students, all the missionaries on furlough, and attend local fellowship meetings. An added bonus was the ability to attend High Street Baptist Church.

## SECOND TERM - ANCHORAGE

Because of health concerns, we decided to locate in Anchorage upon our return to Alaska. We also had found out that in and around Anchorage we could find the greatest number of native people located in one area. Only later did we realize the advantage it was to have lived in a village before attempting to work with the native people in Anchorage. Many times they would come to the "city" and would look us up because they knew we understood village life.

At that time, there was no high school in Bethel or any of the villages. Native teenagers were sent either to Sitka and housed in a dormitory, or others opted to live with "foster parents" in Anchorage for their high school.

I remember taking two or three ladies downtown to Pennys. As we crossed the streets I noticed that they always put me between them and the oncoming cars. Once inside Penny's we decided to take the escalator up to second floor. At the top I looked down and saw that one lady had not gotten on. I had to go back down and bring her up on the elevator.

We started a church right on Fourth Avenue very near downtown. We called it Baptistam Agaayuwik. Translation: Church of God of the Baptists.

We found a property with two log buildings on it. The front building was a small log cabin. (A picture of this little log building is on the front cover.) A larger house was situated behind the smaller one. Lots of repairs had to made, including priming and painting. We used the smaller cabin for services, lived in and had Sunday School classes in the larger house.

Somewhere along the way we acquired a mynah bird. We called the bird "Yaquleq" and taught him to speak in English and Yupik. He would say "Yaquleq asirtuq" which means the bird is a good bird. We had him in a little hallway out of sight of visitors. You should have seen the amazement on the faces of the native people when they would hear this voice saying, "Yaquleq asirtuq." Alas, that bird picked up all the sirens from the fire department and police department. When we had enough of those sirens we agreed to sell him to a native man who offered to reimburse us for what we had paid for him. We learned he was quite an attraction in the village until he grabbed a lit cigarette from an observer. That was the end of Yaqulek. (Later we had a parakeet. We called him Yaquleq as well.)

Fred and Annie Friendly priming the log house

Anna Anvil, husband, daughter

Nice parkas

How well I remember one night that we had a very hard earthquake tremor. I shook Fred and told him we were having an earthquake. He said, "Just go back to sleep – it's probably only a 3 or 4 on the Richter scale." I was very concerned and got up to check on the boys. The next day we found out it was a 5 on the Richter scale. Since then, I have teased Fred that it takes more than a point 5 earthquake to get him out of bed at night!!

The LORD blessed our ministry in Anchorage far above that we could have imagined. As the natives came to Anchorage from their villages they would look us up. We had quite a ministry with the high school students who were boarded in Anchorage.

Because Fred was much better in the Yupik language than I was I decided to enroll in a Yupik Language class offered by Alaska Methodist University. (I believe it goes by another name now.) It was a great help – but I never was as good with the language as Fred was.

There are four men with whom we worked that I would like to tell you about: Elia Michaels, Adolph Friendly, Fred Neilsen, and Jim Rickteroff.

Elia Michaels was from Bethel. (He was actually saved through the ministry of Cecil Owens who took the work in Bethel when we left.) He came in to Anchorage to the hospital because of tuberculosis. He surrendered to preach and was a fiery little preacher. The LORD used him for several years. Later he became backslidden and married a girl that was not a Christian. Sadly he died an early death, probably due in part to drinking.

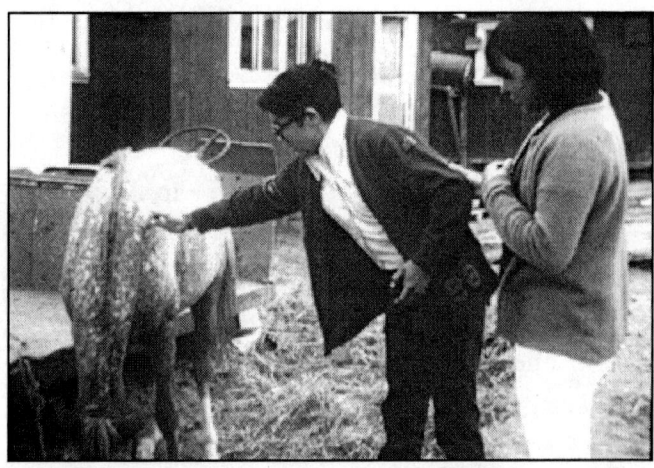

Elia Michael touching a pony that had been flown in to Bethel.

Adolph Friendly was from Quinhagak (on the Kuskokwim River near the southwestern coast of Alaska). He moved to Anchorage. He accepted the Lord's salvation. He and his wife Annie were a great blessing. He was a student of the Word. How well I remember a message he brought on the text: Luke 19:40, **"And he answered and said unto them, I tell you that, if these should hold their peace, the stones would immediately cry out."** (The context was that the Pharisees had told Jesus to rebuke his disciples for loudly praising Him during his triumphal entry into Jerusalem.) At one point his boss told him that he was going to go crazy from reading the Bible too much.

Susan, Annie, Adolph      Fred baptizes Adolph
Friendly

Later while we were in the states on furlough Adolph began drinking again. He and Annie were divorced. He later married Catherine. In the late 90's Adolph had a heart transplant in Salt Lake City. He was in Seattle, Arizona, and Utah for complications and recuperation. He and Catherine stopped in and stayed with us twice when they were down here in the states. He used to play his guitar and sing, "Wasted Years." He told us that he regretted his time away from the Lord. When he finally got right with the Lord it was too late to save his marriage. He passed away in 2008.

Fred and Fred Nielsen          One of the buses for boarding
                               students

Fred Nielsen was from Dillingham and later moved to Anchorage. He had a real desire and commitment to serve the Lord. He was tireless in his visiting, teaching, and praying. He drove one of our buses that picked up high school boarding students for services. He had a very good rapport with the students. On Friday nights we would take the young people to Goose Lake for ice skating. This was an activity enjoyed by all. I believe Fred is currently living in Anchorage. I am not sure of his relationship with the Lord at this time.

Jim Rickteroff was from Nondalton on Lake Iliamna. He came into a service one Sunday evening and was obviously inebriated. At the invitation he came forward and fell upon his knees in repentance. At the time we thought; oh, just another profession that won't last. Actually the Lord moved into his life and, as far as we know, he never drank again. Jim is still serving the Lord with singing and preaching. He was an outcast in his village. He had one leg shorter than the other and the people of the village thought he was devil possessed because of it. He told us that he had slept many nights on the graves of his parents. One of his favorite passages was I Corinthians 1:26-29 **"For ye see your calling, brethren, how that not many wise men after the flesh, not many mighty, not many noble, *are called:* But God hath chosen the foolish things of the world to confound the wise; and God hath chosen the weak things of the world to confound the things which are mighty; And base things of the world, and things which are despised, hath God chosen, yea, and things which are not, to bring to nought things that are: That no flesh should glory in his presence."** He always considered it quite a miracle that God would choose him to preach the gospel. Another Scripture he liked to use was Romans 1:16, **"For I am not ashamed of the gospel of Christ: for it is the power of God unto salvation to everyone that believeth…"**

Jim Rickteroff and John Modig (in glasses)

On one occasion we had what we called a "kuspuk" Sunday. All of the ladies wore their kuspuks. These are loose smock-like dresses used in the summer. Another time we formed a children's kuspuk choir. A native lady and I made kuspuks for the children to wear.

Ladies in kuspuks, I'm third from right

Kuspuk choir

Maggie Lind visited us in Anchorage during the February Fur Rendezvous. She was a joy to be around. She had a very beautiful full length parka that she had made from muskrat stomachs. It was blond in color and very attractive. As she and I made our way walking downtown for the activities we were stopped numerous times by tourists wanting to photograph her. After awhile she confided to me that her smile was "frozen" on her face. Then I began to run interference for her and told some of them that she was just too tired for pictures.

Maggie Lind in her muskrat stomach
parka, church building is just behind her

A dear friend from Quinhagak was named Fanny Fullmoon. Her sister, Emma, had been sent to Sitka for high school. She had never been far from her village and was immensely homesick. She was sent to Anchorage to the Psychiatric Hospital. Fanny and I were dismayed because we both felt that her problem was because of her extreme homesickness. Finally we were able to arrange for her to return to her village if I would escort her there. That was quite a memorable trip in the middle of winter. We flew on several different types of airplanes, from small ones to a cargo flight. When we arrived in the small village I found out that she and her father lived in a one room house. In the middle of the night I had to go to the bathroom. There was a pot in one corner of the room. I waited as long as I could, then swallowed my pride and got up and used the pot. I am sure I was the only one who was embarrassed. After all, it was dark! When I spoke to the village health aide, we both agreed that it would be a good idea to get her weaned off the medication they had prescribed at the hospital. In a few weeks she was doing just fine.

## SECOND FURLOUGH

When it came time for our second furlough we worked out a unique arrangement with George and Anita Ashby. They were willing to come to Anchorage and fill in for us while we were on furlough. They had a home in Springfield, MO. We decided to switch homes for the year. Each of us left our homes fully furnished and we were encouraged to use anything we needed. (Actually the Ashbys got the worse end of the deal. They had a nice home while we lived in the log house on Fourth Avenue.) The Ashbys also had a VW bug which we could use. This was really a blessing for us. (We also inherited a house cat for the year. We didn't realize the cat had fleas until our sons starting getting bites on their legs!!)

We were very concerned for the well being of this cat. All of us left for about a week. We had the cat boarded for the week. When we went to retrieve the cat it ran under an old greasy vehicle. It was covered in dark, oily grease. I don't remember how we got the cat clean. We seemed to be batting zero as far as cats go!

At one point I decided to go to California with Fred. Our friend from High Street (Christina Johnston) agreed to stay with Paul and Ron for a few weeks. Because Fred had more engagements on the west coast, I decided to fly back to Springfield. When I arrived home Christina informed me that I really needed to go grocery shopping. The only problem was that while I was gone the license plates on the VW had expired. Christina said, "Oh, that's okay – just use my car to go to the store." She had a little Dodge Dart; so I thought I could drive that okay. After shopping I returned to her car. It was difficult to get the key in the door lock to open it. Finally I succeeded. The key did not seem to work too well in the ignition either. As I started driving home, it seemed that the car was not shifting into gear as it had on the trip to the store. I thought, "Oh, this is just great! Every time I borrow something there is a problem!"

When I arrived back at the house Christina came out to help me get the groceries in. She took one look at the car and said, "That's not my car!" I was dumbfounded. But she assured me that it was not her car. I quickly went inside and called the grocery store and asked if anyone was missing a car. No one had come forward yet. I told them that if anyone did mention a missing car, please tell them I was on my way back with it. When I got in the car to drive it back I could not get it started with the key I was using. We finally had to get a man from next door to help us get the car going. What a relief when I arrived back at the grocery store. A lady and her daughter were standing there laughing about the whole thing. (It could have turned out worse than that.) It was a relief to get Christina's car back to her. Even to this day I do not like driving someone else's car.

As anyone who has lived in Springfield knows, there are many tornado warnings. There were several times I was scared out of my wits. I didn't dare let the boys know how afraid I was. One time there was a severe tornado heading our way. In my mind the only safe place would be to overturn the sturdy couch and the three of us crawl inside. Fortunately we did not have to follow through with my idea.

A verse that I repeated to myself many times when I was alone at night with the boys was: Psalms 4:8, **"I will both lay me down in peace and sleep, for thou, LORD, only makest me dwell in safety."**

One morning dawned rather chilly. I was trying to impress Paul and Ron that they should dress warmly. I remember telling them that it was 5 degrees. Ron then asked, "Is that 5 degrees hot or 5 degrees cold?" Perhaps he was thinking above or below zero?

At one time we actually planned a week or two of vacation. We told Paul and Ron that we were planning a vacation. The question was posed to us: "Is this a vacation or a trip?" I think they had had their fill of trips and were a little bit leery of this "vacation."

We were visiting mom and dad in Campo, Colorado. Paul and Ron were playing in the back yard. All of a sudden they came running inside and said, "Mom we heard a man shoot at another man, and we saw the fire!!" Actually what had happened was a big clap of thunder and some lightning. (In Alaska we never saw lightning or heard thunder!) We did see some beautiful Northern Lights!

## THIRD TERM – ANCHORAGE

For our third term we returned to Anchorage with the goal of teaching those who wanted to serve the Lord. Fred spent many hours with Adolph Friendly, Fred Nielsen, and Jim Rickteroff – sometimes as a group and sometimes one on one.

At this time we moved to another area of Anchorage so that we could use the larger building for more Sunday School room. Another reason was that while we lived there, it was more or less a fishbowl existence. We realized that our two sons were being subjected to situations that should never have been.

My S.S. class in the log house behind the log church building.

At one point I was asked to write down what occurred during an average day in my life. In response to that request I wrote this poem which says it all. (The words kept coming to me at night. I would get up and go to the bathroom to jot down my thoughts, trying not to awaken Fred. Finally, he asked, "Are you sick or something?")

## A DAY IN THE LIFE OF
## A MISSIONARY WIFE

*To be sure the picture is just right,*
*We shall have to start with the previous night.*
*Two young sons should be early in bed,*
*For the rest that they need, the doctor said.*
*This is always easier said than done –*
*When some sin sick soul needs to be won.*

*I'm not one for complaining; let this be understood –*
*Some need spiritual help, and some need food.*
*Were it not for our wondrous Lord*
*And for the promises and help in His Word,*
*I would be the one in great need –*
*Needing some of that "Precious Seed!"*

*When the last visitor has taken his leave*
*The house may be messy; there is no reprieve.*
*Pick up the toys and papers left lying around,*
*A clean house in the morning should always be found.*
*Cups, saucers, and glasses may be in the sink;*
*It seems most everyone had to have a drink.*

*If we are in bed by twelve or one,*
*We feel a great victory has been won;*
*And then, as likely as not –*
*Someone else has a battle to be fought.*
*The phone may ring at any hour;*

*We usually answer with a word and a prayer.*

*After the phone is hung up, comes a knock at the door*
*Usually a drunk that is wanting some more.*
*Oh! How he needs the Christ that we know.*
*The Love of the Saviour to him we must show;*
*And also the wisdom to turn him away*
*If harm should befall others because of his stay.*

*With children in school there's no sleeping in.*
*That would be quite an outrageous sin!*
*For early callers we must be ready –*
*More problems we perhaps soon shall see.*
*Not all bring problems; some bring cheer*
*And blessing – these make life less drear.*

*Breakfast things all cleared away –*
*Time to start another new day.*
*A prayer for wisdom and grace and love*
*Sent down from the Omniscient One up above.*
*What kind of day is this going to be?*
*Just trust it to the Father – and wait and see.*

*Don't think every day is filled with trouble and strife*
*I wouldn't want to be any other kind of a wife.*
*Sometimes there are blessings that make us forget*
*All the toils and hardships we may have met,*
*And make us rejoice with our new-found friends*

*Over victories won and lives made amends.*

*As a wife, and a mother, and missionary, too;*
*Sometimes 'tis difficult to know just what to do.*
*Which task is most important to Him?*
*We cannot follow our own "little whim."*
*A husband needs his wife; the children need their*
*mother –*
*The people look to the missionary when there is no*
*other.*

*We missionary wives (for myself, mainly, I speak)*
*Are human as you are; and sometimes so weak.*
*"Tis a great measure of patience we need so much;*
*And a look to Him alone, when we need a crutch.*
*Our bodies get weary; and Satan gets busy*
*Trying to get us all in a tizzy!*

*So much seems to hinge on us*
*For added strength from Him, we must trust.*
*There's always the daily chores to be done –*
*And a hundred and more things under the sun –*
*Letters to write; visiting to do;*
*Those at the hospital get so blue.*

*Without His call, I'd never try it;*
*But since He did; I'll not defy it.*
*Let me say once again, just now –*

*The blessings outweigh the trials; and HOW!*
*So, if He should call you; don't be afraid –*
*For you, a door, and a way will be made.*

*You'll be so happy, and rejoice in His call.*
*You'll be a part of His design to tell ALL.*
*You'll go with a prayer and a happy heart –*
*Knowing some day you'll have done your part.*
*So many are waiting yet to be told;*
*Step out, and trust Him; He'll help you be bold.*

*With your husband you'll go to some foreign land,*
*With the Powerful Word of God in your hand.*
*Satan will try to stop you before you start;*
*But just leave it up to the Lord; and take heart –*
*With Him constantly by your side, you can't fail.*
*Over all Satan's darts, with Him you'll prevail.*

We had some great times with the young people who boarded for school in Anchorage. A favorite for everyone was our Friday night ice skating on Goose Lake. (Fred later baptized Annie Friendly in this same lake).

The native girls wore pants almost exclusively. One time a young lady said to me, "I see you always wear a dress or skirt for church." I told her that I thought it showed respect and was more appropriate. The next Sunday she showed up in a very short miniskirt. (I was rather sorry I had encouraged the "skirt!") The weather was usually so bitter cold that we did not make an issue of the dress code.

Early church services in Anchorage

Adolph and Annie Friendly were faithful members of Baptistam Agaayuwik. Annie and I were great friends and had good fellowship. As far as I know, at this writing, Annie is still faithfully serving her Lord. She had such a good attitude and patience. Her mother, Mary Kuku, from Twin Hills, near Dillingham made a beautiful pair of mukluks for me. I still have them and treasure them greatly. (A picture of these mukluks is on the front cover.)

Remember Nellie Forbes, from Bethel? She later moved to Anchorage and was a faithful member of Baptistam Agaayuwik. She brought her sister, Doris, to services. One day after service Doris said to me, "I would like to be baptized." I told her that would be wonderful but she needed to be saved first. We went through the Scriptures about the Ethiopian eunuch. After showing her more verses on salvation, she was saved. She and Nellie still live in Anchorage, but neither of them is in good health.

Another faithful member was Lyda Iyakitan. She was originally from Savoonga on St. Lawrence Island; and former member of Bible Baptist Church in Nome. That is way out north in the Bering Sea. She told us that when she was young she remembered native people coming over from Russia. She made a very authentic Eskimo yoyo for me. Her husband and sons were great ivory carvers. They did not attend services very much.

I almost forgot Mrs. Jacobs, originally from Hooper Bay. She came quite regularly. She was a great basket weaver. I still have one of her baskets. It is very unusual. I have never seen another one just like it, and I have seen many native baskets. It is soft sided and has yarn woven into the sides.

I wish we had kept track of the villages represented by those who visited our services. I am sure it would have been well over 100.

On one occasion Maggie Lind was sent to the Native Hospital in Anchorage. She was quite sick and thinking she might not make it. She called for me and asked me if Fred could administer the last rites for her. (Her background was Moravian and it was hard for her to completely let go of that teaching!) Because she was so sick, I did not want to upset her, but I knew Fred was not about to do that. I just said, "Oh, Maggie, I have assurance from God that you are not going to die." And she lived several more years after this incident.

Another time Maggie came to Anchorage specifically to make a video of Kuskokwim Eskimo legends. It was done at the museum. I am not sure who sponsored it. When she had finished she gave me the ptarmigan feathered headdress that she had used while making the film. I have tried in vain to get a copy of this video.

At one point Fred was asked to teach Yupik to the doctors and nurses at the Native Hospital. He spent several weeks teaching them so that they could communicate better with the natives that spoke that language.

At least on one occasion we joined Bible Baptist Church, of Anchorage, for Youth Camp at Double B Ranch just north of Anchorage. Bro. Don White was pastor at that time. For the first day or two there was quite a lot of friction in my cabin which housed twenty to thirty girls, half of which were native girls. On about the third day the Holy Spirit began to work and many apologies and tears followed. Thank the Lord for the victory in the hearts of these teenage girls. Romans 10:12, **"For there is no difference between the Jew and the Greek: for the same**

**Lord over all is rich unto all that call upon him."**

Double B Youth Camp, combination of Bible Baptist
and Baptistam Agaayuwik

Another time we took some of our native people
to a revival meeting at Bible Baptist Church. When
the invitation was extended my friend, Anna Anvil,
turned to me and said, "I think I need to be saved."
She had been a teacher in the Moravian Church for
many years. But, on that night she told me that no
one had ever told her that she needed to be saved.
She was very happy afterwards and we became
even closer friends than we were before. (There is a
picture of her, her husband, and daughter earlier in
this book.)

We also had a combined Vacation Bible School
one year. Below is a picture of Annie, and some of
the children she taught at that VBS.

I began a teacher training class for those who wanted to teach Sunday School. There were several ladies who attended. Some of them were not members of our church – but I encouraged anyone who wanted to attend. They were able to earn college level credits through Baptist Bible College.

During one of his Bible studies with Adolph and Fred Nielsen, the question was posed to my husband, "What is the Scriptural example that you and your wife follow in being missionaries.?" After a very thorough search of the Scriptures, they decided that we really had no Scriptural example. Aquila and Priscilla were fellow helpers to Paul, but never ventured out on their own to another land. The example they found was that the disciples were sent out two by two. They were sent as soldiers and were not to be encumbered with wives, children and the mundane things of this world. This was very contrary to anything we had ever heard or been taught. Yet, we could not deny the examples given in the Bible. The Mormons practice this method with great success. While I do not agree with their doctrine in any way, perhaps they do have the right method. (This is the reason we left Alaska as missionaries and came to Washington state.)

If you are interested in further search into this topic you may visit the website of our mother church: Calvary Independent Baptist Church. The website is: **http://idahobaptist.com**. Then click on the link in the lower left corner, **Books and Articles**. Look for the article entitled, *The Missionary Dilemma.*

I will just summarize our ministry after leaving Alaska. Fred taught in a mission school called Northwest Baptist Missions in Pasco, WA. The focus was to teach those who had a burden for people of the north. After a year or two, he became pastor of Tri-Cities Baptist Church (also in Pasco). He pastored that church for about 25 years. In 2004 he resigned because he felt he was not able to do all that he should be doing as a pastor. Our church people did not necessarily feel that way and did not want him to resign. It was a difficult decision. The people of that church were wonderful to us, and we greatly miss them. They voted him Pastor Emeritus. In October of 2010, Fred began services in Finley (near Kennewick) as Calvary Independent Baptist Mission. (Several people had asked him if he would be willing to teach them.) At the ripe old age of 78, he is at it again. We got so tired of hearing preachers get up and give a verse or two of Scripture and then give about 30 minutes of stories. Another reason for this venture is that we are more convinced in the absolute sovereignty of God. Even though most people say they believe they are saved by grace, many of them think they have just a little part (in saying a prayer, or whatever). Salvation is wrought by conviction of the Holy Spirit and is totally of God. As the Scripture says, we are literally raised from the dead. Ephesians 2:1,4, and 5; **"And you *hath he quickened,* who were dead in trespasses and sins ... But God, who is rich in mercy, for his great love wherewith he loved us, Even when we were dead in sins, hath quickened us together with Christ, (by grace ye are saved;)"** Can a dead person do anything?

## ADDITIONAL PICTURES OF INTEREST

Sketch of church done by Adolph Friendly
Notice caribou antlers at the back

Boarding students on bus to church

Additional picture of children taken to VBS at Bible Baptist Church Fred is at right

Musicians - (The Eskimo people are very talented in music. I never met one who could not sing well!) Many of them could play the guitar

Group of preachers - Top row, left to right: Visiting preacher, Allen Swires, visiting preacher, Fred Nimmo, Dick Swanson Jim Rickertoff is to the right of Dick Swanson in dark jacket. In the middle are Adolph Friendly and Fred Neilsen  Paul is on left and Ron is on the right in the front

Paul and Ron with friends in tree fort

Furlough family picture - Paul is on the left, Ron is on the right

Ron in our yard when we lived on 4th Avenue (Downtown Anchorage)

# Anchorage Daily Times

ANCHORAGE, ALASKA, MONDAY, APRIL 23, 1962

## Native Language Kept Aliv[e]

By HELEN GILLETTE
Times Staff Writer

When people quit talking a language, it dies, and this, linguists agree, is what will soon happen to the various Eskimo and Indian languages.

But in his own small way, one fairly new Alaskan is doing what he can to hold back this fateful day.

He's the Rev. Fred Nimmo, Baptist missionary who is holding language classes at the Alaska Native Medical Center for staff and patients and anybody else who's interested.

The basic purpose of the class, held with the cooperation of the rehabilitation project at the hospital, is to assist doctors and other staff members in talking to their various native patients.

The class, which has diminished as students realized it was going to be real work, meets every Thursday at 4:30 p.m. in the hospital solarium.

Quick to admit that he's no linguist, the Rev. Mr. Nimmo of unbounded enthusiasm for the native tongues.

"They're really tremendous languages, he said. "They carry many more shades of meaning than English has. You can say what you mean with much more exactness."

Aside from giving the doctors and nurses a small working knowledge in the native tongues, Nimmo likes to teach the Eskimo people how to write their own language.

Although the language is so difficult to master, natives who know how speak it readily learn to write it, he said.

The minister, who says his motivation encourages Alaskan missionaries to work with the people in their own language, got his basic knowledge from the University of

Alaska at Fairbanks about five years ago.

Actually, the regular course was finished at the time, and he worked with a tutor connected with the school.

After that he and his wife, Winora, were based at Bethel where he continued trying to learn as much language as he could directly from the people.

While at Bethel, he became acquainted with an old man who showed him what he called the ancient writing of his people.

"I have often read," he said, "that the Eskimo languages

were only spoken language till missionaries and reduced them to writing around the turn of the centu[ry].

"But my experience must, and with others, to believe that the Es[kimo] a written form [of] that."

Last fall the mission was transferred to A[nchorage] He is beginning to [hold] weekly church service[s in] Yupik dialect (spoken Bethel area), at his rabic church at 430 F[...]

Right now he has Testament in the translation and a bit which he wrote as the salvation" to serve [a] material for those ser[...] plans to write more tra[...] native language, with of native translators him with form and w[...] of meaning.

Right now Rev. Nim[mo] not encourage beginner[s] his hospital langua[ge] which got underway in [...]

But if there should mand, he will be glad mand, for a beginner's class, body who's interested.

As for himself, Rev. enjoys talking to the old men in a language "th[at's] to their heart." He f[inds] his mission work in thi[s] effective when he can [...]

As for his family, Wi[th] their two little boys, five, and Ronnie, thr[ee] the language too.

At the hospital, the said he much enjoys with the personnel of habilitation departmen[t] including Stewart Rauls[...] rector, Miss Flora J[...] Miss Letha Mullin, and his nurses.

"It would be wonde[rful] minister said, "he kne[w] of these languages aliv[e for] other generation."

**NIMMO FAMILY STUDIES THE LANGUAGE**

Members of the Rev. Fred Nimmo family study details of the complex Eskimo and Indian languages at their Anchorage home. The family members, all of whom speak some of the language, are children Ronnie, 2, and Stanley, 3, and Rev. Nimmo's wife, Winona.

To box 24)
Bethel, A. A. A.
Dec. 16, '64

Dear Rev Nimmo;

Hope you are fine. I'm fine. School is fine and so I am to. On the 14th of December we were invited to a dinner at Marie Gridley's home at the Native Hospital and there was Mrs. Scot, Mrs. Walker, Mrs. Manley, Marie Gridley, Mrs. Nimmo, Stanly, and I. also while we were there Eva Boyce gave a present to Mrs. Nimmo, Stanly, and I. Stanly had a Alaska Coloring Book and Mrs. Nimmo had perfume, earres, and a pin then me was Avon perfume. On the December 15th at night your wife teached me to become a christian cause I wanted to be a christian. Tell your friends I said "Hello" to them and Ronnie. May God Bless you all.

Sincerely Yours, Peggy Moses

Our 50th Anniversary picture taken in March 2010

## ADDENDUM

I would like to say that I feel very blessed for having been able to spend a few years with the native people of Alaska. I would not trade anything for the experience. We found them to be very hospitable and gentle. We made many lasting friends. Both Fred and I are so thankful that the LORD allowed us to go to Alaska.

As we were going over the editing of my book, a friend asked me about the story knife. I decided to give a little explanation of it.

As I was walking along (in Bethel) one day, I noticed two little girls playing in the wet sand. As I came closer, I asked them what they were doing. Their response was that they were telling stories. Each girl had a table knife in her hand. They took turns telling stories. As they related the story they sketched scenes in the sand. (Some of the mothers told me that it was hard to keep table knives because they kept disappearing for story telling!)

Years ago the storytellers had knives made out of ivory especially for the times when they wanted to tell their stories. You rarely see a genuine ivory story knife nowadays. You see a picture of my story knife in this book. The only other one that I have seen that compares to this knife was at the museum in Anchorage.

This next excerpt is one of Maggie Lind telling

the Eskimo legend: "How the Crane Got its Blue Eyes".

## HOW THE CRANE GOT ITS BLUE EYES

Nunam qainga mamkillrani (a long time ago on earth) we the humans and the animals spoke the same language and could understand one another.

This story was passed from Crane to our people a long time ago. A long time ago Crane was sitting with a group of Yupik (real people) and he told this story. During berry season, I had been flying for a long, long time, I decided to stop by a slow moving river and eat. I was sooo tired and hungry and the berries looked so good. Before I started eating, I looked around. The sky was blue, only a hint of clouds in the sky, the river was quiet and nobody or nothing was around me. I felt safe. I decided that I wanted to concentrate only on eating today, as I had been flying for many days and was very very hungry. So instead of watching for danger while eating - I decided that I would just take out my eyes, put them on a stump and have them watch out for danger for me. I took out my eyes and holding them in my hands, I told them "I am going to go eat berries; watch and call me if you see danger". My eyes said, "Yes master". Then I put them on a stump facing the river. I went about eating blueberries, and felt my way into the cranberries. Just then I heard

"Master, Master come quick I see danger!" So I went back to the stump as fast as I could and put my eyes back in and looked around, - the sky was clear, the river was quiet and all I saw was this stick floating slowly down the river. I was angry and scolded my eyes, "There is no danger - I see nothing!" Still angry I put my eyes back on the stump and said, "Now watch for danger - and do not bother me if it is only a stick floating down the river!" I went back to the spot where I remembered the blueberries; I moved on and found salmonberries. Ooh they were small and so sweet; the juice was wonderful, so I decided to go further and found a patch of blackberries. They too were good. All of a sudden all sound around me went quiet - and I heard my eyes calling "Master, master come quick; master we are in danger; MASTER!" I was in the middle of eating some juicy berries so I called, "What do you see?" My eyes said, "Something is floating down the river; master come quick!" Thinking about the stick from before, I slowly turned around and made my way back to the stump - but without eyes this took a long time. Meanwhile, I heard my eyes calling "Master help us" over and over. When I got to the blueberries the sound started to grow faint - getting further and further away! I found the stump and my eyes were gone! I should have listened, I cried, "What am I to do without eyes?" I could not see the fox or the wolves. Then it came to me; the berries were round like my eyes -- why not use them?  So I felt around. Without my eyes I was blind. I found two nice round berries and put them where my eyes used to be - they were blackberries. I looked up and the sky was black, the sun was black; it was like night. This would not do - so I took them out and stumbled on to where the cranberries were. I found two nice round cranberries and put them where my eyes used to be and looked up; everything was red. The sky was red, the river was red and the tundra was red. I did not like that so I took them out and went on with my search. I came upon some salmonberries and put them where my eyes used to be and looked around. Everything was orange; the sky was orange, the clouds were orange, the water was orange. I did not like the salmonberries for eyes.  I journeyed on and came upon some blueberries - I found two nice round ones. I put them where my eyes used to be and looked up and everything was beautiful, the sky was blue, the water was blue and everything looked just right.

Now that is why the Crane has Blue Eyes!

*Story as told by Maggie Lind*
*Bethel, Alaska*
*1964*

*There are two morals to this story:*
  *1. Never put onto someone else or something else*
  *what you could do yourself and*
  *2. Always listen to your body!*

**Winene Nimmo**

*joyni3237@gmail.com*
*509-545-4637*